LIZ EARLE'S
QUICK GUIDES

Vitamins & Minerals

LIZ EARLE'S
QUICK GUIDES

Vitamins & Minerals

BOXTREE

ADVICE TO THE READER

*If you suffer from any physical disorder or special conditions, please
consult your doctor before taking vitamin or mineral supplements.*

First published in Great Britain in 1994 by Boxtree Limited,
Broadwall House, 21 Broadwall, London SE1 9PL

The right of Liz Earle to be identified as Author of this Work has
been asserted by her in accordance with the Copyright, Designs and
Patents Act 1988

10 9 8 7 6 5 4 3 2 1

ISBN: 1 85283 989 9

Text design by Blackjacks
Cover design by Hammond Hammond

Printed and bound in Great Britain by
BPC Paperbacks Ltd

A CIP catalogue entry for this book is available from
the British Library

Contents

Acknowledgements

I am grateful to Valerie Holmes and the Vitamin E Information Service and also to Dr Derek Shrimpton for technical expertise; also for the invaluable information from Boots Micronutrients Information Service. I am also indebted to the talented team at Boxtree, and to Rosemary Sandberg and Claire Bowles Publicity, for their unfailing enthusiasm and support.

The RDA references are from the *Report on Health and Social Subjects 41. Dietary Reference Values for Food Energy and Nutrients for the United Kingdom. A Report of the Panel on Dietary Reference Values of the Committee on Medical Aspects of Food Policy* (COMA), 1991.

Food values are from McCance and Widdowson, *The Composition of Foods*, 5th edition, Royal Society of Chemistry, Ministry of Agriculture, Fisheries and Food. With additional information from the 1993 United States Department of Agriculture Database.

Abbreviations

g   gram

mg   milligram (one-thousandth of 1g)

mcg   microgram (one-thousandth of 1mg, one-millionth of 1g)

RDA   Recommended Daily Amount (this Government guideline is the level just above the minimum needed to prevent serious deficiency)

RNI   Reference Nutrient Intake (these amounts are the same values as RDAs and the two are interchangeable. RNI is a term which is increasingly used by nutritionists)

Introduction

New research is proving that vitamins and minerals play a vital part in living a longer, healthier life. Not only can many nutrients help to prevent serious diseases, they can also promote the body beautiful and encourage greater well-being. This book will give you all you need to know about vitamins and minerals, as well as many other important nutrients. With the help of this book you will discover how the latest nutritional research will work for you and your family. So many of us now feel the need to take vitamin and mineral supplements to improve our health and vitality, but it is important to know exactly what to take. It is also essential that we have a guide to dosage and safety. For these reasons, this book also includes information on safe supplementation for all ages.

Liz Earle

1
Vital Vitamins and Minerals

There's no doubt that vitamins and minerals are an integral part of our well-being and play a vital role in the complex biochemical jigsaw that goes on inside our body. Boosting our intake of vitamins and minerals goes a long way to protect the body from many of the side-effects of modern living. Exciting new research also now suggests that antioxidants such as beta-carotene, vitamin C and vitamin E can help protect us from some of the biggest killers in Western society, such as coronary heart disease. Nutritionists are recognizing that a healthy diet does not necessarily supply all of the vital nutrients that today's hectic lifestyle demands. Leading experts believe that we should pay special attention to the unique action of antioxidants, while not forgetting the importance of many other better-known vitamins and minerals.

Why do we need nutrients at all? On a scientific level, some vitamins and minerals are needed for chemical reactions such as releasing energy from food or breaking down fat molecules. Others build strong bones, keep the skin supple and help protect us against stress or pollution. Scientists have discovered a close link between antioxidant nutrients and the ageing process. Although these are no magic elixir of youth, some nutrients may even hold the power to slow down skin ageing and keep us feeling young. This book takes a close look at the role of vitamins and minerals and reveals how they can be of benefit. At every age, throughout every day, a good supply of nutrients holds the key to improved health and well-being.

Eat Well – Stay Healthy!

The idea that a well-balanced diet, full of vitamins and minerals, is essential for a healthy body is nothing new. The message for us all to eat more healthily has rung out loud and clear for several years now – so why the enormous growth in the sales of vitamin pills? It seems that despite being more aware about the foods we should be eating, few of us actually put healthy eating into practice. Today, we tend to rely on highly processed foods because they are easy and convenient. Few of us have the time or energy to spend much time shopping, preparing and cooking fresh wholesome foods. All too often our requirement for vitamins and minerals is forgotten in our food and it may be easier (and can be cheaper) to take supplements.

But although vitamin and mineral supplements can be useful, they are no substitute for a good diet. There are several very good reasons why we should all aim to eat more healthily. Foods contain much more than just vitamins and minerals – they also contain substances such as enzymes and fibre which are not found in ordinary vitamin pills. Eating a well-balanced diet that is rich in wholesome, natural foods keeps our weight down and increases our energy levels. Good food is a form of preventative medicine in itself and helps maintain our health throughout childhood, adolescence, adulthood and beyond into old age. Nutrition experts agree that one of the keys in good nutrition is to increase the amount of fruit and vegetables in our diets. How much do we need? The answer is probably a good deal more than we are getting at the moment! Most of us actually eat *less than half* the amount of fruit and vegetables recommended by the World Health Organization. This authority suggests eating *at least* 400g (almost 1lb) every day, excluding potatoes. In other words, we should eat a minimum of five generous portions of fruit and vegetables each day. How many of us can claim to do this every day of the week? Very few indeed. This brings us back to one reason why so many of us are turning to a daily multivitamin supplement for nutritional security. Although vitamins and mineral tablets are no substitute for a healthy diet they can be a very useful optional extra.

Vitality Eating Goals

By following these simple guidelines for a well-balanced diet we automatically increase our intake of valuable vitamins and minerals.

* Less fat – especially the saturated type found in meat, cream and cheese. Trim all visible fat from meat and hide the frying pan.
* Less sugar – especially the simple (refined) sugars added to processed foods.
* Less salt – watch out for salted snacks and never add salt to food at the table.
* Less alcohol – cut back in general and aim for several alcohol-free days a week.
* More fruits and vegetables – aim to eat five generous portions per day (not including potatoes, which count as starches).
* More low-fat foods – switch to low-fat yoghurt and low-fat fromage frais instead of full-fat varieties or cream. Use skimmed or semi-skimmed milk.
* More complex carbohydrates – eat more wholegrains, wholewheat pasta and brown rice.
* More fluids – drink more water and diluted fruit juices, such as apple, orange and carrot juice.

Healthy-eating Food Pyramid

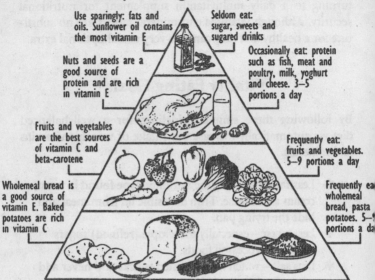

Use sparingly: fats and oils. Sunflower oil contains the most vitamin E

Seldom eat: sugar, sweets and sugared drinks

Nuts and seeds are a good source of protein and are rich in vitamin E

Occasionally eat: protein such as fish, meat and poultry, milk, yoghurt and cheese. 3–5 portions a day

Fruits and vegetables are the best sources of vitamin C and beta-carotene

Frequently eat: fruits and vegetables. 5–9 portions a day

Wholemeal bread is a good source of vitamin E. Baked potatoes are rich in vitamin C

Frequently eat wholemeal bread, pasta potatoes. 5–9 portions a day

Pyramid Portions

Protein:

> one portion = 3oz/75g lean meat or fish; 2 eggs; 10oz//300g cooked beans or lentils; 1/3pint/200ml semi-skimmed or skimmed milk; small pot of yoghurt or fromage frais; 1/2oz/40g cheese

Fruits and Vegetables:

> one portion = 1 teacup filled with chopped fruit or vegetable; 1 piece of fruit e.g. apple, orange, banana; potatoes do not count as a vegetable here as they are starchy foods

Complex Carbohydrates:

> one portion = 1 slice wholemeal bread; 1 heaped table-spoon cooked rice, pasta or grains; 3 1/2oz/90g cooked potatoes

How Vital Vitamins are Lost

A delicious, nutritious variety of fresh fruits, vegetables and wholegrains are the key vitamin-rich ingredients of any well-balanced diet. But we do need to take care to preserve their vitamin values. Unfortunately it is not enough just to stock up the larder with fresh foods – we must look after it too. Avoid storing fresh produce for long periods of time as their vitamins diminish with age. Chop vegetables just before you cook them, as exposing their cut surfaces to the air reduces many nutrients. The water-soluble vitamins such as vitamin C and the B complex vitamins are easily lost as they dissolve in the boiling liquid. Although vegetables are a good source of vitamin C, we often end up tipping a good deal down the sink. So eat fruit and vegetables raw whenever possible, or cook without water by steaming, stir-frying or briefly cooking in the microwave.

Many minerals are also lost during food preparation and processing. Some calcium and iron is lost in the cooking water, but they are far more likely to be depleted by foods with high levels of oxalic acid (found in chocolate and rhubarb) and phytates (found in cereals, especially bran). Large amounts of minerals are lost during food refining. Believe it or not, about 80 percent of zinc disappears in flour milling and 50 percent is removed during rice polishing. The answer is to eat wholewheat flour and brown rice. There are other advantages to eating unrefined foods too, as brown rice has fifteen times the selenium content of polished rice and wholemeal bread has twice the selenium found in white bread.

—2—
Do You Get Enough?

The amount of vitamins and minerals needed by individuals on a daily basis is a matter of some debate. It is also a complex issue and one on which even the foremost nutrition experts cannot agree. Most countries in the world have devised a system of Recommended Daily Amounts (RDAs). These are not necessarily the amounts we should be aiming for in our diet, but are just above the bare minimum needed to prevent serious illness due to a deficiency. For example, too little vitamin C will result in scurvy, a life-threatening illness that used to kill several thousand sailors set at sea without any vitamin C from fresh fruit. The RDAs for vitamin C ensure that we will not develop scurvy, but are not enough to give us additional antioxidant protection.

The Issue of RDAs

The RDAs of vitamins and minerals are arbitrary amounts that vary widely between countries. They do not exist for every vitamin and mineral, even though each nutrient is essential for life. Here in the UK we fall some way behind the Americans, who generally have RDAs at levels about one-third higher than are advised in Britain. Some of the Scandinavian and Russian RDAs are higher still – so who is right? The answer is that no one really knows. Nutritional research has come such a long way in the last few years that the goal posts are constantly changing. However, one thing is clear. Taken in sufficient quantity, some nutrients have the ability to help prevent disease and maximize our well-being. These are the kinds of levels that we should be aiming for. In most cases we can do this by eating a well-balanced diet, but in a few cases we may need to rely on supplements. This view is accepted by the Government and there are several official recommendations for some people to take supplements on a daily basis, notably iron and folic acid (see in Vitamins and Minerals on pages 18 and 33).

In addition, our Recommended Daily Amounts are likely to rise in the future. A recent meeting of the National Academy of Sciences in America has decided that the time has come to take a closer look at raising RDA vitamin and mineral levels. This powerful scientific board conducts reviews of nutritional standards and the last general review was in 1989. It has since announced that due to the tremendous advancement in nutritional research there is now a substantial need to review the position of nutrition – especially in the light of recent antioxidant research. For the first time in history, this prestigious board is talking in terms of setting higher levels of vitamin and mineral RDAs for optimizing health as distinct to the lowest levels needed to prevent illness from a deficiency. With this in mind, the review panels in the United Kingdom are currently looking at whether we should be getting far more vitamins and minerals in our diet than was previously thought necessary.

When using this quick guide as a reference book, keep in mind that the current RDAs of many vitamins and minerals do not take into account the latest nutritional findings, nor the new demands placed on our bodies by factors such as pollution and over-refined diets. As we have seen with vitamin C, the RDA is based on preventing scurvy and does not address the very useful role of vitamin C as an antioxidant in helping to prevent disease. Even senior scientists have questioned the low levels of RDAs. As an example, Professor Anthony Diplock, Head of Biochemistry at Guy's Medical School, now advises a daily dose of 100–150mg of vitamin C every day, more than four times the official RDA. Professor Diplock also suggests daily levels for other nutrients, including beta-carotene and vitamin E, neither of which currently have an official RDA. Remember that the issue of our current RDAs is not about good health, it is about the minimums needed to prevent disease. What is more relevant is the level of nutrition that we should aspire to in our diet in order to promote good health.

Safety First

Whenever the subject of taking vitamin and mineral supplements is mentioned there is the obvious question of safety. There have been many scare stories in the press in recent years about the safety of some vitamins. It is important to put these into perspective. The vitamins and minerals present in many types of food occur naturally in our diet. They have played an important part in mankind's development for thousands of years and are safe substances to take in the normal amounts available to maintain and encourage better health. The same cannot be said for many of the common prescription drugs used to treat disease. All drugs have side-effects and many are highly toxic. *Studies show that vitamins are 1,000 .imes safer than drugs.* In a recent five-year period, no fatalities due to taking vitamin supplements were reported to the American Poison Control Centers. By contrast, during the same period, drugs of all kinds caused at least 1,200 accidental deaths.

All substances are toxic, it is just a question of the amount taken. For the record, taking large quantities of fat-soluble vitamins, such as vitamin A or D, will cause reversible liver damage – but taking excess quantities of a substance as common as paracetamol will cause irreversible liver damage and death. Both kinds of tablets are available in every high street chemist. In this quick guide you will find toxicity details as they are known beside every major nutrient listed. This gives you an idea of how poisonous, or not, the nutrient is. The majority are extremely safe even in very high doses; however, it is important to make note of the exceptions. It is also vital to appreciate the difference between an adult dose and those given to children. Keep supplements in a child-proof container when possible and store out of the reach of children. Finally, always read the label on the bottle and never take more than the stated recommended dose. It is also advisable to consult your GP if in any doubt, although bear in mind that during their many years of medical training most doctors spend only a few hours studying the basics of nutrition. For more technical expertise it may be worth consulting a qualified nutritionist and details on how to do this are given at the end of this book. Doctors may be unaware of many of the more important research findings, or be unnecessarily dismissive of nutritional therapy to prevent disease.

—— 3 ——
A–Z of Vitamins

Vitamins are chemically complex substances which we must obtain from many different foods in order to survive. Although we only need tiny amounts of vitamins they are all vital for our health and well-being. They have many hundreds of uses within the body and low levels can lead to ill-health, serious diseases or even, in extreme cases, death.

VITAMIN A (RETINOL)
This fat-soluble vitamin can be stored in the body. It is sometimes referred to as the 'skin vitamin' as it is needed to repair skin tissues and low levels lead to spots, acne and a scaly scalp. Vitamin A is essential for healthy eyes and helps us to see in dim light. It is also needed for an improved immune system, for healthy growth in the young, for strong hair and nails. There are two forms of this valuable nutrient: retinol, which comes from animal produce such as cod liver oil, liver, eggs and butter, and the 'precursor' to vitamin A called beta-carotene, found in brightly coloured fruits and vegetables. Basically, beta-carotene is converted into vitamin A as it is needed. This means that even vegetarians who do not eat animal produce need not worry about running low on vitamin A.

Best sources: Cod liver oil, liver, kidney, eggs and dairy produce such as milk and butter.

Depleted by: Cooking (especially when in contact with iron and copper utensils) and exposure to the air.

Deficiency: Symptoms of low levels include skin infections, dry skin and scalp, poor eyesight – especially in low light levels, headaches and dry eyes. Severe deficiency leads to xeropthalmia (drying and degeneration of the eye's cornea) and night blindness.

Daily needs: The official British RDA is as follows: babies under one year 350mcg, one–six years 400mcg, seven–ten years 500mcg; females from eleven years onwards 600mcg, during pregnancy 700mcg, during breast feeding 950mcg; males eleven–fourteen years 600mcg, from fifteen years onwards 700mcg.

Toxicity: Huge doses of a synthetic form of vitamin A (tretinoin) have been linked to a few isolated cases of birth defects in the USA. For this reason the British Government advises that pregnant women limit their intake of vitamin A. However, it should be noted that this nutrient is essential for the correct development of the unborn child. The amount of liver eaten by pregnant women should also be reduced (liver contains a large amount of vitamin A – 13,000mcg to 40,000mcg per 100g, depending on the type). Regular intakes should not exceed 7,500mcg in adult women and 9,000mcg in adult men. Children are more sensitive and daily intake should not exceed 900mcg in babies, 1,800mcg for one–three years, 3,000mcg for four–six years, 4,500mcg for six–twelve years and 6,000mcg for teenagers. Doses above these amounts should only be taken under supervision.

Supplements: Most supplements of vitamin A (retinol) contain between 2,500mcg (7,500IU – international units) and 6,000mcg (18,000IU – international units). Beta-carotene is a safer supplement to take and provides the body with all the vitamin A it is likely to need.

BETA-CAROTENE

This nutrient is technically not a vitamin but it is converted by the body into vitamin A when we run short. Any beta-carotene left over is used in the body as an antioxidant (see The Antioxidant ACE Vitamins on page 57). This means that it controls the formation of free radicals, the destructive particles that damage cells and lead to disease. Many important studies around the world have shown that high intakes of beta-carotene are linked to low levels of certain types of cancer. Beta-carotene also protects the skin from sun damage and may be given as a treatment for sun-induced skin itching and swelling.

Best-sources: Carrots are by far the best source of beta-carotene in our diet. Tomatoes, watercress, broccoli, spinach, mangoes, pumpkin, cantaloupe melon and apricots and other colourful fruits and vegetables are all excellent sources.

Depleted by: Exposure to sunlight. Beta-carotene is very stable during cooking and its levels may actually increase. This is because beta-carotene is released from the cell walls of vegetables as they are cooked and softened.

Deficiency: Those who do not eat large quantities of colourful fruits and vegetables are likely to have low levels in their diet.

Daily needs: There is no official British RDA for beta-carotene, but to get maximum antioxidant protection many experts are advising a level of around 15mg daily.

Toxicity: There is no known toxicity of this nutrient, although mega-doses will turn the skin a pale shade of yellow. For this reason, high doses of beta-carotene can be found marketed as tanning pills.

Supplements: Most supplements of beta-carotene contain between 3mg and 15mg. The natural source of beta-carotene (from *Dunaliella salina* algae) is believed to be more easily absorbed by the body.

B COMPLEX VITAMINS

These water-soluble vitamins are not stored by the body and so we need a constant supply every day. Several nutrients make up the vitamin B complex family. They work in synergy with each other and so should always be taken together in supplements, unless you are professionally advised otherwise.

VITAMIN B1 (THIAMINE)

Needed for the release of energy from food. Thiamine is the most unstable member of the vitamin B complex family. Essential for the digestion, the nervous system and for helping us cope better with stress.

Best sources: Offal, pork, milk, eggs, wholegrain cereals, brown rice, barley, fortified breakfast cereals.

Depleted by: Food refining, heat and cooking. Also lost in the water drips from frozen food, so save the thawed liquid when defrosting. Also depleted by alcohol and indigestion (antacid) medicines.

Deficiency: Signs of low levels include tiredness, nausea, loss of appetite, irritability and depression. Extreme deficiency leads to the fatal disease beriberi, common in Third World countries.

Daily needs: The official British RDA is as follows: babies under one year 0.3mg, one year onwards 0.4mg. There are known to be increased needs during pregnancy and breast feeding, and at times of illness and stress. Alcohol drinkers and the elderly also have increased needs for thiamine.

Toxicity: Non-toxic.

Supplements: Most supplements contain between 10mg and 75mg.

VITAMIN B2 (RIBOFLAVIN)

Involved in energy metabolism and the development of healthy skin, hair and nails, riboflavin is destroyed by sunlight. More than half the riboflavin content of milk will be lost after two hours' exposure (so don't leave it on the doorstep for too long). Riboflavin is widely used as a yellow food-colouring ingredient.

Best sources: Milk, eggs, fortified bread and cereals, green leafy vegetables, lean meat (especially liver) and fish.

Depleted by: Sunlight, alcohol, smoking and oestrogen-based drugs such as the contraceptive pill.

Deficiency: Signs of low levels include cracked and sore lips, inflamed tongue, bloodshot or sore eyes, scaling skin, insomnia and dizziness.

Daily needs: The official British RDA is as follows: babies under one year 0.4mg, one–three years 0.6mg, four–six years 0.8mg, seven–ten years 1.0mg; females from eleven years onwards 1.1mg, during pregnancy 1.4mg, during breast feeding 1.6mg; males eleven–fourteen years 1.2mg, from fifteen years onwards 1.3mg. Extra supplies are also known to be needed by alcohol drinkers, smokers and those taking oestrogen-based drugs such as the contraceptive pill.

Toxicity: Even at high doses side-effects are virtually unknown.

Supplements: Most supplements contain between 10mg and 75mg.

VITAMIN B3 (NIACIN)

Also known as nicotinic acid. The body converts this to niacinamide (nicotinamide) which is used to break down fats and create energy. High doses may also protect the insulin-producing cells of the pancreas. Clinical trials are currently underway to determine whether supplements of nicotinamide can help prevent diabetes. Niacin has also been shown to lower blood cholesterol and other blood fats and may be recommended in treatment for the prevention of heart disease.

Best sources: Meat, fish, wholegrain cereals, eggs, milk, cheese and fortified breakfast cereals.

Depleted by: Food refining. Stable during cooking but lost in water drips when thawing frozen foods. Also depleted by alcohol, smoking and oestrogen-based drugs such as the contraceptive pill.

Deficiency: Mild symptoms include muscle weakness, loss of appetite and digestive disorders. Extreme deficiency leads to a disease called pellagra, characterized by rough, scaling skin.

Daily needs: The official British RDA is as follows: babies under six months 3mg, seven–nine months 4mg, ten–twelve months 5mg, one–three years 8mg, four–six years 11mg, seven–ten years 12mg; females eleven–fourteen years 12mg, fifteen–eighteen years 14mg, nineteen–fifty years 13mg, during pregnancy 15mg, fifty years onwards 12mg; males eleven–fourteen years 15mg, fifteen–eighteen years 18mg, nineteen–fifty years 17mg, fifty years onwards 16mg. Alcohol drinkers also require extra supplies.

Toxicity: High doses cause changes in liver functioning. Doses of nicotinic acid (not nicotinamide) in excess of around 200mg daily can cause temporary flushing, reddening of the skin and pounding headaches. Higher doses cause a temporary lowering of blood pressure.

Supplements: Most supplements contain between 25mg and 125mg.

VITAMIN B5 (PANTOTHENIC ACID)

Another B vitamin that is involved with the release of energy from fats and carbohydrate. Also involved with the body's immune system and healthy tissues, including the skin. Needed to convert choline into acetylcholine, an important substance used by the brain.

Best sources: Yeast, liver and other offal, eggs, brown rice, wholegrain cereals and molasses.

Depleted by: Light and heat (including cooking), caffeine, alcohol, sulphur and oestrogen-based drugs such as the contraceptive pill.

Deficiency: Signs of low levels may include prematurely greying hair and hair loss.

Daily needs: No official British RDA.

Toxicity: No toxic signs after daily doses of 10g for six weeks, although levels this high may cause stomach upsets.

Supplements: Most supplements contain between 25mg and 250mg.

VITAMIN B6 (PYRIDOXINE)

Used in protein and amino acid metabolism. Also helps make healthy red blood cells and regulates the nervous system. This B vitamin is used to combat skin inflammations and maintain healthy teeth and gums.

Best sources: Meat, fish, milk, eggs, wholegrain cereals (especially wheatgerm) and vegetables.

Depleted by: Cooking, food refining, alcohol and oestrogen-based drugs such as the contraceptive pill.

Deficiency: Low levels can lead to dermatitis-like skin conditions, loss of appetite and leg cramps. Severe deficiency may cause a burning sensation in the feet. Those with high protein diets are at greater risk of a deficiency due to its reaction with amino acids in protein.

Daily needs: The official RDA is as follows: babies under six months 0.2mg, seven–nine months 0.3mg, ten–twelve months 0.4mg, one–three years 0.7mg, four–six years 0.9mg, seven–ten years 1.0mg; females eleven–fourteen years 1.0mg, fifteen years onwards 1.2mg; males eleven–fourteen 1.2mg, fifteen–eighteen years 1.5mg, nineteen years onwards 1.4mg. Increased needs during pregnancy and breast feeding, also for women taking the contraceptive pill. Alcohol drinkers, smokers and those under stress also have increased requirements.

Toxicity: Low toxicity. Some side-effects reported at doses of between 100mg and 500mg.

Supplements: Most supplements contain between 25mg and 200mg.

VITAMIN B9 (FOLIC ACID)

This works in tandem with vitamin B12 to create new cells. Low levels lead to anaemia. Folic acid is essential for women from the moment they conceive as it can help prevent spina bifida in the first twelve weeks of pregnancy. Women planning to become pregnant can ask their GPs to prescribe folic acid supplements in order to reduce their chances of having a baby with spina bifida. The Department of Health has made these supplements available to women, although details do not appear in the doctor's drug manual *MIMS* or the *British National Formulary*, making it hard to prescribe. Folic acid also helps make RNA and DNA and aids the transmission of our genetic code.

Best sources: Offal, green leafy vegetables, wheatgerm, nuts, eggs, fortified bread, bananas, oranges and pulses such as lentils.

Depleted by: Light, heat (including cooking, although it is protected by the presence of vitamin C), food refining, alcohol and oestrogen-based drugs such as the contraceptive pill.

Deficiency: Low energy levels and fatigue, irritability and confusion. Persistent shortfall can lead to megaloblastic anaemia, where red blood cells have a shorter lifespan.

Daily needs: The official British RDA is as follows: babies under one year 50mcg, one–three years 70mcg, four–six years 100mcg, seven–ten years 150mcg; females eleven years onwards 200mcg, during pregnancy 300mcg, during breast feeding 360mcg; males eleven years onwards 200mcg. Dramatically increased needs during the early weeks of pregnancy to protect the development of the foetus; also in the later stages of pregnancy to prevent anaemia and during breast feeding. Increased requirements for smokers, alcohol drinkers and the elderly.

Toxicity: Low toxicity. High doses may cause insomnia and interfere with zinc absorption.

Supplements: Most supplements contain between 50mcg and 400mcg.

VITAMIN B12 (COBALAMIN)

Essential for the formation of red blood cells and low levels will be seen as a type of anaemia (pernicious anaemia). This vitamin also maintains our nervous system and helps give us energy. It is the only vitamin to contain a mineral element (cobalt).

Occasionally given as an injection or as a nasal gel which is reputed to boost energy levels.

Best sources: Animal products such as liver and other kinds of offal, eggs, cheese, milk, meat and fish. Vegetarians should eat yeast extracts, such as Marmite, or seaweeds and algae such as kelp and spirulina which are also rich in vitamin B12.

Depleted by: Light and heat (including cooking), alcohol and oestrogen-based drugs such as the contraceptive pill.

Deficiency: Low levels can lead to a pale, grey or yellow complexion and hair loss.

Daily needs: The official British RDA is as follows: babies under six months 0.3mcg, seven–twelve months 0.4mcg, one–three years 0.5mcg, four–six years 0.8mcg, seven–ten years 1.0mcg; females eleven–fourteen years 1.2mcg, fifteen years onwards 1.5mcg, during breast feeding 2.0mcg; males eleven–fourteen years 1.2mcg, fifteen years onwards 1.5mcg. Alcohol drinkers and smokers also need extra supplies. Vegetarians and vegans may need to take a supplement as vitamin B12 is commonly found only in animal produce.

Toxicity: Non-toxic. Injections of as much as 3g daily are reported to be safe.

Supplements: Most supplements contain between 10mg and 100mg.

BIOTIN

Not a true vitamin, but works with the B complex family. Biotin is a water-soluble co-enzyme that can be made by microbes in the intestines, as well as being found in many common foods. It is essential for breaking down and metabolizing fats in the body and is important for healthy skin tissues.

Best sources: Offal, eggs, milk and dairy products, cereals, fish, fruit and vegetables (notably cauliflower and mushrooms).

Depleted by: Leaching into the cooking water and food refining. Also reduced by the presence of raw egg white which contains a protein that attacks biotin.

Deficiency: Low levels can lead to dermatitis and a scaling scalp. Those taking antibiotics or with digestive disorders will have reduced levels.

Daily needs: No official British RDA. Our needs are increased when stressed or taking antibiotic drugs.

Toxicity: Non-toxic. Daily doses of 10–200mg officially reported to be safe and adequate.

Supplements: Most supplements contain between 25mcg and 500mcg.

CHOLINE

This is also not a true vitamin as a certain amount can be made in the liver from protein, especially the amino acid called methionine. Choline functions as a basic constituent of lecithin and this is also its richest source. Choline is needed to metabolize fats within the liver, for the efficient transmission of nerve impulses and for the nervous system.

Best sources: Offal, egg yolk, lecithin, wheatgerm, brewer's yeast, nuts, pulses and oranges.

Depleted by: Relatively stable during cooking and storage.

Deficiency: Low levels may lead to increased blood fats and nerve damage. Those on a low-protein diet may be deficient.

Daily needs: Not known. However a balanced diet should aim to contain 200–1,000mg. No official British RDA.

Toxicity: Low toxicity even at high doses.

Supplements: Most supplements contain between 25mg and 200mg.

VITAMIN C (ASCORBIC ACID)

This water-soluble nutrient is not stored by the body and so we need a constant daily supply. It is essential for healthy connective tissues such as the skin and walls of blood vessels. Low levels of vitamin C lead to internal bruising, poor healing of wounds and bleeding gums. Vitamin C is an important antioxidant (see

The Antioxidant ACE Vitamins on page 57). This means that it controls the formation of free radicals, the destructive particles that damage cells and lead to disease. Studies show that those who eat large amounts of vitamin C may be better protected from some kinds of cancer and heart disease.

Vitamin C is more effectively absorbed from the diet when eaten with bioflavonoids (also known as vitamin P). These are substances that are naturally present in foods rich in vitamin C (eg the pith of oranges contains bioflavonoids). The main bioflavonoids are rutin, hesperidin, citrin and flavonoids. Some bioflavonoids also have an antioxidant action.

Best sources: Fruits and vegetables, especially blackcurrants, oranges, broccoli, cabbage and potatoes.

Depleted by: Light and heat (including cooking), re-heating foods, smoking and caffeine.

Deficiency: Early deficiency signs include bleeding gums and poor hair growth. Low levels lead to poor wound healing and reduced antioxidant protection. Extreme deficiency results in the fatal disease scurvy.

Daily needs: The official British RDA is as follows: babies under one year 25mg, one–ten years 30mg; females eleven–fourteen years 35mg, fifteen years onwards 40mg, during pregnancy 50mg, during breast feeding 70mg; males eleven–fourteen years 35mg, fifteen years onwards 40mg. Smokers are recommended to add at least 80mg to these figures. Many experts now suggest that the official RDAs should be raised to at least 100mg, with further increased needs during pregnancy and breast feeding. Smokers should also supplement their diet as each cigarette has been estimated to destroy approximately 25mg of vitamin C.

Toxicity: Non-toxic even at high doses. Very high levels can cause diarrhoea. High doses may lead to kidney stones in those with unusually high oxalate levels. However, this risk is statistically small.

Supplements: Most supplements contain between 50mg and

2,000mg. Many vitamin C supplements include rosehip concentrate, a rich source of bioflavonoids, to aid absorption.

VITAMIN D

These fat-soluble vitamins work together with calcium to keep blood and bones healthy and strong. Children who do not get enough D vitamins develop a bone deformity called rickets. Low levels of vitamin D in adults also lead to a bone disease called osteomalacia.

Best sources: Animal produce such as milk and eggs, oily fish such as mackerel, butter and cheese. Cod liver oil is a rich source. Vitamin D is also made by the action of sunlight on the skin. Synthetic vitamin D is added to margarine.

Depleted by: A relatively stable vitamin.

Deficiency: Low levels in childhood lead to rickets and bone deformities. In adults, low levels can cause softening of the bones and osteoporosis. Asian children and women who cover themselves when outside, or those who are house-bound, may risk a deficiency as they do not absorb enough sunlight through the skin to manufacture vitamin D.

Daily needs: The official British RDA is as follows: babies under six months 8.5mcg, seven months to three years 7mcg; females during pregnancy and breast feeding 10mcg, males and females 10mcg after the age of sixty-five. In the USA a daily amount of 10mcg is recommended throughout life.

Toxicity: The most toxic of all the vitamins. Side-effects from more than 50mcg taken daily. The highest permitted dose (without prescription) in UK supplements is 10mcg daily.

Supplements: Most supplements contain between 200 and 400IU (international units) or/5–10mcg.

VITAMIN E (TOCOPHEROL)

This fat-soluble vitamin has many varied and widespread functions throughout the body and protects cells from damage.

Vitamin E helps reduce the risk of blood clots, strengthens blood vessels, increases muscle strength and influences hormones. In addition, vitamin E is a powerful antioxidant (see The Antioxidant ACE Vitamins on page 57). This means that it controls the formation of free radicals, the destructive particles that damage cells and lead to disease. Those with a high daily intake of vitamin E have been found to be better protected from some kinds of cancer and heart disease.

Best sources: Vegetable oils (especially unrefined sunflower and rapeseed oils), almonds, peanuts, sunflower seeds, avocado, asparagus, spinach and other green leafy vegetables.

Depleted by: Food refining, light and air.

Deficiency: It is hard to assess vitamin E deficiency as there are no outward signs. Low levels may lead to serious diseases, including some kinds of cancer, arthritis, cataracts and heart disease. However, as these tend to be slowly progressive, the symptoms may not appear until after many years of consistently low levels of vitamin E in the diet.

Daily needs: No official British RDA. Our needs depend upon the amount of polyunsaturated fats eaten in the diet. Many experts are now recommending a guideline of 50–80mg (75–20IU). Clinical anti-cancer trials in the USA have involved doses of up to 800IU daily, with no reported side-effects.

Toxicity: Non-toxic even in high doses.

Supplements: Most supplements contain between 100 and 400IU which is equal to around 60–250mg, depending on the type of vitamin E used. Natural vitamin E is more potent than the synthetic form.

VITAMIN K1

These fat-soluble vitamins are essential for normal blood clotting. Vitamin K1 injections are routinely given to newborn babies to help prevent internal bleeding and haemorrhage. However, there has been a reported link between these and an increased incidence of childhood leukemia. At present there are no official guidelines but some health authorities are now giving vitamin K1 drops orally instead.

Best sources: Widely available in vegetables such as cauliflower, Brussels sprouts, cabbage, spinach, peas and wholegrain cereals.

Depleted by: Light, food refining and deep freezing.

Deficiency: Possible in newborns due to poor transfer across the placenta and low levels in breastmilk, so nursing mothers should increase their supplies. Antibiotics can also lead to a deficiency.

Daily needs: No official British RDA. Increased needs for newborns, those with liver diseases or those taking antibiotics or anticoagulant drugs.

Toxicity: Non-toxic in its natural form. The synthetic form of menadione is best avoided as it has been linked to liver damage in the newborn.

Supplements: Not commonly available in supplement form.

CO-ENZYME Q10

Also known incorrectly as vitamin Q or ubiquinone, from the Latin word meaning 'everywhere'. Although the body can make its own supply (so this nutrient is not technically a vitamin) this ability declines with age. Co-enzyme Q10 is found in the mitochondria, the powerhouses of most of our cells. When the immune system is protecting the body against a virus or invading bacteria, it demands more energy. Co-enzyme Q10 helps provide this energy. It has a direct action on the immune system by creating more energy for the cells and the theory is that this makes them more effective. Co-enzyme Q10 serves the same purpose as the cylinders in a car engine, where the petrol is ignited and explodes to drive the piston. Without this nutrient, the body is like a dead engine as there is no ignition spark. Co-enzyme Q10 is also an important antioxidant (see The Antioxidant ACE Vitamins on page 57) and helps prevent the oxidation of fats within the system.

Best sources: It is thought to be present in many foods, but these have not yet been analysed.

Depleted by: Food refining.

Deficiency: Low levels can cause the heart to malfunction. Supplements are being used in clinical trials to treat heart disease. Low levels are also found in diabetics and patients with muscular dystrophy.

Daily needs: No official British RDA. The body's needs are believed to increase with age.

Toxicity: Not known. Therapeutic doses of 100mg have been used daily with no reported side-effects.

Supplements: Supplements are taken by over twelve million people in Japan as they are said to help every cell in the body release energy. Most supplements contain between 10 and 30mg and this upper level is the amount currently being used in medical trials.

—4—
A–Z of Minerals

As with vitamins, we need small but essential amounts of minerals every day. Minerals are single chemical elements which are involved in many different processes within the body. They are naturally present in the soil where they are taken up by plant roots, passing through the food chain to end up in fruits, vegetables and animals. The amount of minerals in our food depends on the quality of the soil in which they are grown. Organically grown crops are known to contain higher levels of many essential minerals. Minerals are divided into two groups – major minerals and trace elements. This does not mean that the major minerals are more important – simply that the body requires a greater quantity.

BORON
This mineral is plentiful in the earth's crust and is becoming popular as a bone-strengthening supplement. It is claimed to help prevent osteoporosis and arthritis but the evidence is not conclusive. American researchers suggest boron acts as a gate-keeper for oestrogen, the natural hormone that helps to lay down calcium and maintain healthy bones. It may play a role in balancing oestrogen and testosterone, hence its potential for helping menopausal and post-menopausal women.
Best sources: Root vegetables grown in boron-rich soil.
Depleted by: Food refining.
Deficiency: No specific cases of boron deficiency symptoms.
Daily needs: No official British RDA. Daily requirements have not been established, but the average diet probably contains around 2mg boron.

Toxicity: Symptoms of toxicity appear at doses of around 100mg. Mega-doses of 15–20g can be fatal.

Supplements: Bone-strengthening supplements aimed at menopausal women usually contain between 1 and 3mg. Boron supplements should be balanced with calcium, magnesium and vitamin D to boost absorption.

CALCIUM

Almost our entire calcium supply can be found in our teeth and bones. The calcium content of our bones varies from day to day as it is released into the bloodstream and replenished from food. The tiny amount left over is needed for healthy muscle contraction and blood clotting. Calcium relies on vitamin D to be used properly. Low levels of vitamin D also lead to a calcium deficiency. Calcium is most commonly extracted from limestone, although sea water is also a good source. Dolomite is another more absorbable and inexpensive form of calcium.

Best sources: All dairy products, especially cheese, yoghurt and fromage frais. Also green leafy vegetables, broccoli, hard tap water, the bones of tinned fish (such as salmon and sardines), peanuts and sunflower seeds. Skimmed milk contains slightly more calcium than full-fat varieties.

Depleted by: Phytates present in whole grains, especially bran fibre, which bind with calcium making it unavailable to the body. Only 20–30 percent of our total calcium intake is absorbed and utilized. Phosphorus (found in all fizzy drinks) also prevents calcium from being properly used.

Deficiency: Low levels are often found in those with a high phosphorus intake. Deficiencies are possible in those who lack the lactose-digesting enzyme which aids calcium absorption. Anyone on a dairy-free diet should consider taking calcium supplements. This is especially important for children and for women during pregnancy or breast feeding. Menopausal women have increased needs as circulating oestrogens reduce calcium levels in the bones. This can lead to osteoporosis (brittle bones) and dowager's hump. Hormone replacement therapy (HRT) may help prevent this.

Daily needs: The official British RDA is as follows: babies under twelve months 525mg, one–three years 350mg, four–ten years 550mg; females eleven–eighteen years 800mg, nineteen years onwards 700mg, during breast feeding 1,250mg; males eleven–eighteen years 1,000mg, nineteen years onwards 700mg. Children have high demands for calcium as bone deposits are laid down in early years. Our best bone density is achieved at around thirty–five years of age. This then declines and we all lose about 0.3 percent per year. This calcium loss increases in women after the menopause. Absorption of calcium also decreases with age, so our needs are raised in later life.

Toxicity: Low toxicity as excess calcium levels are automatically monitored by the body's filtering system. However, high doses of vitamin D can lead to calcium being deposited in the kidneys. This condition can be fatal so it is especially important not to over-supplement with vitamin D.

Supplements: Most supplements contain between 200 and 900mg. Calcium is often taken with vitamin D to facilitate absorption.

MAGNESIUM

This is used in the transmission of nerve impulses which is why it is sometimes known as an anti-stress mineral. It can help fight depression and keep the circulatory system healthy. Magnesium is stored in the bones and soft body tissues. It works together with calcium and the two minerals should be kept in balance with each other. Recent studies show that it may help prevent disorders as diverse as heart disease and pre-menstrual tension.

Best sources: Soya beans, nuts, wholegrain cereals, meat, fish (especially seafood) and figs.

Depleted by: Phytates present in whole grains and bran fibre bind with magnesium making it less available to the body. High levels of phosphorus, calcium, vitamin D and fats all interfere with its absorption.

Deficiency: Low levels are rare as it is widely available. It is lost during illness when their is a high fever, vomiting or diarrhoea.

Daily needs: The official British RDA is as follows: babies under three months 55mg, four–six months 60mg, seven–nine months 75mg, ten–twelve months 80mg, one–three years 85mg, four–six years 120mg, seven–ten years 200mg; females eleven–fourteen years 280mg, fifteen–eighteen years 300mg, nineteen years onwards 270mg, during breast feeding 320mg; males eleven–fourteen years 280mg, fifteen years onwards 300mg.

Toxicity: Low toxicity. Signs of over-use at doses of 3–5 g daily for long periods include reddening of the skin and excessive thirst.

Supplements: Most supplements contain between 200 and 500mg.

PHOSPHORUS

Around 80 percent of the body's phosphorus is found in our bones. The remaining amount is vital for converting food into energy. Because of its role in strengthening our bones, we should eat twice as much calcium as phosphorus.

Best sources: Widely available in dairy produce, vegetables, fish, meat, nuts and wholegrains so a deficiency is unlikely.

Depleted by: Very little. A stable mineral.

Deficiency: Rare as phosphorus is widely available in foods and routinely used in many food additives.

Daily needs: The official British RDA is as follows: babies under one year 400mg, one–three years 270mg, four–six years 350mg, seven–ten years 450mg; females eleven–eighteen years 625mg, nineteen years onwards 550mg, during breast feeding 990mg; males eleven–eighteen years 775mg, nineteen years onwards 550mg.

Toxicity: Toxic in large amounts. High levels in the diet interfere with the absorption of calcium and can lead to weakened bones.
Supplements: Supplements are not necessary.

POTASSIUM, SODIUM AND CHLORIDE

These minerals are known collectively as electrolytes. They are essential in body fluids and are involved in a wide range of biochemical processes. We lose these minerals via perspiration, so athletes, manual workers or those living in hot climates may need to replace their electrolytes with special drinks or dietary supplements.

Best sources: Common table salt which is added to most manufactured foods provides sodium, but it is important not to eat too much salt (sodium) as it can easily overload the kidneys. Potassium is found in yeast, fruits and vegetables. Chloride is found in yeast, bacon and smoked fish.

Depleted by: Potassium can be lost in cooking; however, these three minerals are comparatively stable.

Deficiency: Unlikely, as all three minerals are plentiful in most foods. Extra supplies might be needed after unaccustomed vigorous exercise as these minerals are lost in sweat.

Daily needs: The official British RDA for sodium is as follows: babies under three months 210mg, four–six months 280mg, seven–nine months 320mg, ten–twelve months 350mg, one–three years 500mg, four–six years 700mg, seven–ten years 1,200mg; males and females age eleven onwards 1,600mg.

The official British RDA for potassium is as follows: babies under three months 800mg, four–six months 850mg, seven–twelve months 700mg, one–three years 800mg, four–six years 110mg, seven–ten years 2,000mg; males and females eleven–fourteen years 3,100mg, fifteen years onwards 3,500mg.

The official British RDA for chloride is as follows: babies under three months 320mg, four–six months 400mg, seven–twelve months 500mg, one–three years 800mg, four–six years 1,100mg, seven–ten years 1,800mg; males and females eleven years onwards 2,500mg.

Toxicity: High levels of any of these three minerals lead to kidney problems. Each nutrient interacts with the others so supplementing one can cause an imbalance. Toxicity side-effects reported with potassium at intakes above 17g.

Supplements: These are not generally necessary. Some specialist sports drinks contain a combination of these minerals to replace those lost during exercise.

——— 5 ———
A–Z of Trace Minerals

Although we only need tiny amounts of trace minerals they are just as important for good health as the major minerals and vitamins. These nutrients are also known as trace elements.

IRON

About half of our body's iron is in the form of haemoglobin, the substance that gives blood its red colour. Haemoglobin carries oxygen from the lungs around the body, so low iron levels cause tiredness and muscle fatigue. Iron is also needed for muscle protein and is stored in organs such as kidneys and liver. If our diet does not contain enough iron, these stores will be used up and anaemia will result. Iron is lost in blood and women can lose a significant amount during a menstrual period. High iron levels can lead to potentially damaging free-radical activity. Calcium and copper must be present in order for iron to function effectively within the body.

Best sources: Liver and kidney as well as other forms of meat are rich in iron. Bread, fortified breakfast cereals, beans, nuts and green leafy vegetables also provide useful amounts, although we absorb less iron from non-meat sources. Iron is present in food in both organic (haem) and inorganic (non-haem) forms. Haem iron is found in meat and is easily absorbed. Non-haem iron found in vegetables must be reduced to the ferrous form by vitamin C before it can be absorbed.

Depleted by: Iron is relatively stable. However, caffeine interferes with its absorption.

Deficiency: Low levels are characterized by pale skin and pale inner eyelids, which are classic signs of anaemia. Other signs of low levels include tiredness, lethargy, poor vision, indigestion and tingling in the fingers and toes. Iron deficiency (anaemia) is common during and after pregnancy and should be checked by a blood test in routine ante- and post-natal care. Iron needs rise dramatically during pregnancy as the foetus takes up almost half the woman's daily iron supplies.

Daily needs: The official British RDA is as follows: babies under three months 1.7mg, four–six months 4.3mg, seven–twelve months 7.8mg, one–three years 6.9mg, four–six years 6.1mg, seven–ten years 8.7mg; females eleven–fifty years 14.8mg (acknowledged to be insufficient for women with heavy periods who lose a great deal of iron this way. The RDA advisory panel agree that the most practical way of meeting iron requirements is for these women to take supplements.), females fifty years onwards 8.7mg; males eleven–eighteen years 11.3mg, nineteen years onwards 8.7mg.

Toxicity: High doses can cause stomach pains and constipation. Supplements should not be given to children (as little as 3g can be fatal for a small child). A dose of around 100g is lethal for adults.

Supplements: Most supplements contain between 5 and 25mg.

CHROMIUM

This is involved in the metabolism of carbohydrates and fats and is also involved in the production of insulin. High levels of sugars in the diet stimulate the excretion of chromium via the kidneys. For some unknown reason, Oriental races have more than twice the chromium content in their skin and bones compared to Europeans.

Best sources: Yeast, egg yolk, liver, wheatgerm, cheese and wholegrain cereals. Alcohol also contains chromium.

Depleted by: Food refining (80 percent is lost from wholewheat flour when it is turned into white; raw sugar loses 98 percent when refined into white granulated sugar).

Deficiency: Low levels cause blood sugar irregularities and may play a part in diabetes. High sugar levels in the diet may lead to a deficiency. Signs of low levels include mental confusion, irritability, depression, learning difficulties and excessive thirst.

Daily needs: No official British RDA. A safe and adequate level is believed to lie above 25mcg for adults. Less than 10 percent of our daily chromium is actually absorbed and used by the body. Our ability to absorb and store chromium declines with age, so more may be needed by the elderly.

Toxicity: Low toxicity, partly because so little of it is absorbed.

Supplements: Chelated chromium supplements are better absorbed than most. The best forms of chromium to take are picolinate and amino acid chelate. Most supplements contain between 25 and 100mcg.

COPPER

This is an essential component of many of the body's enzymes and is also involved with forming red blood cells. Copper also functions as an antioxidant as it is a component of many enzymes present in cells, including superoxide dismutase (SOD), which combats free radicals. Many who have arthritis maintain that wearing a copper bracelet reduces pain and inflammation of the joints. This may be because traces of copper dissolve through the skin and are absorbed into the bloodstream.

Best sources: Liver, crab, oysters, nuts, wholegrain cereals, lentils, olives and carrots. Copper also reaches our diet through pesticides in foods, liquids stored in copper containers and copper water pipes.

Depleted by: Very few factors. A stable nutrient.

Deficiency: Signs of low levels include pale skin, prominent veins and diarrhoea. Extreme deficiency can lead to brittle bones, greying hair and low white blood cell count leading to poor resistance to infections. Low copper levels are rare as it is a common mineral.

Daily needs: The official British RDA is as follows: babies under three months 0.2mg, four–twelve months 0.3mg, one–three years 0.4mg, four–six years 0.6mg, seven–ten years 0.7mg; females eleven–fourteen years 0.8mg, fifteen–eighteen years 1.0mg, nineteen years onwards 1.2mg, during breast feeding 1.5mg; males eleven–fourteen years 0.8mg, fifteen–eighteen years 1.0mg, nineteen years onwards 1.2mg.

Toxicity: Low toxicity except at high levels when symptoms can include nausea, abdominal pain and mental disturbances. Excess copper intake is harmful and high blood copper levels are seen in some cases of epilepsy and heart disease. Tap water from copper piping may produce high levels in the body, upsetting the balance of other nutrients. Run the tap for thirty seconds before using the water to clear any residual traces. High copper levels are reduced by vitamin C and the minerals manganese and zinc.

Supplements: Most supplements contain between 1 and 3mg. Many multi-mineral supplements do not contain copper as an excess is harmful and it is widely present in our diet.

IODINE

This is best known for regulating the thyroid gland that controls our metabolism and counters weight gain. It controls the production of hormones including thyroxine and tri-iodothyronine. These control the body's metabolic rate – the speed at which oxygen is burned in the body to release energy. This also controls the growth of children. Iodine is also an important antidote to low levels of nuclear fallout and radiation sickness.

Best sources: Seafood, fish, kelp and seaweeds.

Depleted by: Low levels in the soil lead to vegetables and other crops with a low iodine content. Eating vegetables from the brassica family of greens (cabbage, broccoli, etc), maize, bamboo shoots, sweet potato and lima beans can all interfere with the uptake of iodine. Many prescription drugs also prevent its absorption.

Deficiency: Low levels are rare unless no sea produce is eaten. Extreme deficiency causes goitre or an underactive thyroid, a common condition in underdeveloped countries.

Daily needs: The official British RDA is as follows: babies under three months 50mcg, four–twelve months 60mcg, one–three years 70mcg, four–six years 100mcg, seven–ten years 110mcg; males and females eleven–fourteen years 130mcg, fifteen years onwards 140mcg. There are increased needs for iodine during pregnancy and breast feeding.

Toxicity: Moderate level of toxicity and the safe upper limit should not exceed 17mcg per kilo of body weight daily. This means not more than 1,000mcg for the average adult. However, daily doses should not exceed 250mcg daily unless under professional guidance. Iodine may worsen some cases of dermatitis.

Supplements: Natural-source iodine is extracted from seaweed. Most supplements contain between 25 and 250mcg.

MANGANESE

This is essential for normal growth and development. It helps create the protective glycoprotein coating around cells. It is also needed in the body to make the natural anti-viral agent *interferon* and to help regulate blood sugar levels. Manganese also functions as an antioxidant as it is part of the enzyme called superoxide dismutase (SOD). This enzyme combats free radicals. It is also needed for the body to be able to use vitamins C, E and the B complex vitamins.

Best sources: Oats, wheatgerm, nuts (especially almonds and hazelnuts), wholegrain cereals, pineapples, plums, beans, beetroot and dark lettuces.

Depleted by: Food refining (less than one–sixth of the manganese found in wholemeal flour is found in refined white flour).

Deficiency: Low levels are rare as it is widely available; however, only a small percentage of manganese is absorbed from the diet.

Daily needs: No official British RDA. Those who eat plenty of whole grains and nuts are unlikely to be deficient. However, those with excessive copper levels may run short of manganese as the latter is used by the body to prevent copper damage. It is also present in tea and those who drink six or more cups a day are getting useful levels (although the caffeine content of tea interferes with the absorption of other nutrients).

Toxicity: Low toxicity. High levels may lead to lethargy and muscle disorders.

Supplements: Most supplements contain between 3 and 20mg. The best forms to take are amino acid chelate and gluconate as these are more easily absorbed by the body.

MOLYBDENUM

Most of our molybdenum is stored in the liver and it is used to metabolize iron. It has diverse functions and helps prevent tooth decay and impotence. Molybdenum also assists with the removal of excess copper levels from the system.

Best sources: Buckwheat, pulses, wheatgerm, liver, soya beans, barley, lentils, rye, eggs, wholewheat pasta and bread.

Depleted by: Food refining and food grown on poor soil.

Deficiency: Low levels are rare but the signs include irritability and irregular heartbeat.

Daily needs: No official British RDA, but the USA recommends 30–300mcg for children depending upon age and 150–500mcg for adults.

Toxicity: Low toxicity. High levels can cause gout (10–15mg a day) and increased excretion of copper, resulting in a copper deficiency.

Supplements: Most supplements contain between 5 and 500mcg.

SELENIUM

As rare as gold and just as precious to the body. Selenium is vital as an antioxidant and works in conjunction with vitamin E. It forms an integral part of the free-radical scavenging enzyme glutathione peroxidase, which has an important antioxidant action. It is also needed for the body's manufacture of proteins, keeps the liver functioning healthily and boosts the immune system. Selenium is also a component of sperm and plays a role in fertility. It also helps remove heavy metals from the body, including cadmium and mercury (essential if you are a smoker).

Best sources: Yeast, garlic, eggs, liver and fish. Animal produce is generally richer in selenium than vegetables – especially when they have been grown in poor soil.

Depleted by: Intensive farming and fertilizers on the soil, smoking.

Deficiency: Symptoms include chest pains, hair loss and low resistance to disease. Studies show our daily selenium levels are falling due to over-farmed soil resulting in nutrient-depleted crops.

Daily needs: The official British RDA is as follows: babies under three months 10mcg, four–six months 13mcg, seven–twelve months 10mcg, one–three years 15mcg, four–six years 20mcg, seven–ten years 30mcg; females eleven–fourteen 40mcg, fifteen years onwards 60mcg, during breast feeding 75mcg; males eleven–fourteen years 45mcg, fifteen–eighteen years 70mcg, nineteen years onwards 75mcg. The World Health Organization advises 50–200mcg daily.

Toxicity: Highly toxic in large doses. Selenium poisoning is unlikely to occur from food but could happen if too many supplements are taken. Daily intake should not exceed 450mcg for adult males (roughly equivalent to 6mcg per kilo of body weight, daily). Side-effects have been reported at intakes above 750mcg daily. Signs of nail damage have been seen in adults taking 900mcg daily.

Supplements: Selenium yeast or amino-acid based supplements are preferable to selenite tablets as they are less toxic. Most supplements contain between 50 and 250mcg and are often combined with other antioxidant nutrients, such as vitamins C and E to increase its efficacy within the body.

SILICON

Also known as silica, this is the second most plentiful element on the planet after oxygen. It forms long complex molecules, hence its structural role in plants such as bamboo which need to be long, supple and strong. In humans, silicon is a small but vital part of all connective tissues, bones, blood vessels and cartilage. It may play a role in preventing osteoporosis (brittle bones) by assisting the utilization of calcium within the bones. Silicon also helps strengthen skin, hair and nails by improving the production of collagen and keratin.

Best sources: root vegetables and other forms of plant fibre, organically grown fruits and vegetables (grown in nutrient-dense soil), brown rice and hard drinking water.

Depleted by: Food refining and chemical fertilizers in the soil.

Deficiency: Clinical signs of deficiency are not known. Low levels in the diet may lead to weakened skin tissues. The levels of silicon in our skin decrease with age.

Daily needs: No official British RDA. Our daily requirements are not known but may be between 20 and 30mg.

Toxicity: Low toxicity.

Supplements: Natural supplements are extracted from bamboo or horsetail plants. Most supplements contain between 2 and 400mg.

SULPHUR

A little-known trace element that helps create healthy, supple skin. Sulphur is needed to form keratin, the protein found in our joints, hair and nails. It also plays an important role in the structure of almost all proteins and enzymes found in the body. Hair contains significant amounts of sulphur (curiously, curly hair has more than straight). Sulphur is found in other nutrients, including the amino acids cysteine and methionine, and the B complex vitamins thiamine and biotin.

Best sources: Shellfish, beef, eggs, chicken, pork, dried peaches, pulses (especially kidney beans) and peas. All high-protein foods contain sulphur.

Depleted by: Food refining.

Deficiency: Low levels are unlikely in those eating good quantities of protein.

Daily needs: No official British RDA. Our daily requirements are not known.

Toxicity: Intakes above 0.7mg of pure sulphur daily are believed to overload and damage the small intestine. However, taking high levels of organically complexed sulphur (such as amino acids) have not been shown to be toxic.

Supplements: Most supplements contain between 6 and 20mg of organically complexed sulphur. Amino acid-based supplements are the safest form to take.

ZINC

Most of our zinc is stored in our bones, but it is needed for more than eighty enzyme activities throughout the body, such as red blood-cell production. Zinc acts as an internal traffic controller, directing and maintaining the flow of body processes and cell maintenance. Low levels in children stunt growth and reduce the appetite. One-fifth of the body's zinc supplies can be found in the skin and it is used to assist tissue repair. Trials have shown zinc supplements to be as helpful as some antibiotics in treating skin conditions such as acne. A sign of zinc deficiency is losing the sense of taste. Zinc is also believed to have an antioxidant function and supports the other antioxidant nutrients.

Best sources: Widely available in offal and other meats, mushrooms, oysters, yeast, eggs and mustard.

Depleted by: Food refining and processing (brown rice contains six times more zinc than polished white varieties). Phytates in cereals such as wholewheat and bran fibre bind with zinc, making it unavailable to the body.

Deficiency: Low levels have been associated with a low sperm count, birth defects and hyperactivity in children. Many factors decrease zinc levels in the body, including the contraceptive pill, steroids, smoking and alcohol. The average diet supplies between 10 and 15mg zinc, of which only 20 percent is absorbed by the body.

Daily needs: The official British RDA is as follows: babies under six months 4mg, seven months to three years 5mg, four–six years 6.5mg, seven–ten years 7mg; females eleven–fourteen years 9mg, fifteen years onwards 7mg, during breast feeding 13mg; males eleven–fourteen years 9mg, fifteen years onwards 9.5mg. Vegans may benefit from a supplement as they do not eat the common animal produce rich in zinc.

Toxicity: Low toxicity. Doses of 50mg a day may interfere with the metabolism of both iron and copper. Up to 150mg daily has been used therapeutically under professional guidance. Prolonged doses of 75–300mg daily are associated with copper deficiency and a form of anaemia. Mega-doses of 2g or more cause nausea.

Supplements: Most supplements contain between 10 and 30mg.

——6——
A–Z of Amino Acids

The amino acids are the unsung heroes that make up every type of protein in food. Traditionally, nutritionists only worried about whether a protein was 'complete' or not. This means whether or not it contains all of the essential amino acids in adequate quantities. Now, individual amino acids have been highlighted for their own therapeutic effects and this is a new and exciting area of nutritional medicine. Around twenty amino acids have been identified to date, and of these nine cannot be made by the body. These nine amino acids are termed 'essential' as it is vital that we obtain them from our food. However, protein supplied in food can be difficult to break down into the individual amino acids. Each one plays a specific part in maintaining health. They are all found in high levels in protein foods, including meat (especially game, chicken and pork), wheatgerm, oats, eggs and dairy produce (especially cottage cheese and ricotta cheese).

The following are the nine essential amino acids:

CYSTEINE
Required to absorb selenium and protect the body from pollution. It also contains sulphur which is needed to control blood sugar levels and create collagen. Supplements are not recommended for diabetics except under medical supervision.

ISOLEUCINE
For healthy haemoglobin production and skin growth. A deficiency in animals induces tremors and muscle twitching.

Low levels of isoleucine have been found in anorexia nervosa patients.

LEUCINE
Lowers blood sugar levels and promotes rapid healing in skin and bones. Found to be lacking in both drug addicts and alcoholics.

LYSINE
Required to make collagen in the skin. Has been shown to inhibit the growth of viruses and may help control the herpes simplex (cold sore) virus. High levels are found in nuts and seeds.

METHIONINE
One of the most important 'anti-ageing' nutrients as it is involved with producing nucleic acid, the regenerative part of collagen. Good sources include beans, pulses, garlic, onions and eggs.

PHENYLALANINE
Regulates the thyroid gland and helps control the skin's natural colouring through the pigment melanin. Sometimes used therapeutically as an anti-depressant and to increase assertiveness. Reputed to be an appetite suppressant and painkiller. Some people are fatally allergic to phenylalanine, so it should always be listed on the label when added to food and drinks. Pregnant and breast feeding women are advised to avoid phenylalanine.

THREONINE
Found in high levels in infant blood plasma to protect the immune system. Regulates neurotransmitters in the brain and fights depression. Some studies indicate it may help reduce wheat intolerance.

TRYPTOPHAN
Used as a natural sleeping pill as it has tranquillizing properties. Tryptophan is broken down into serotonin, a neurotransmitter responsible for sending us to sleep. One of the best sources is peanuts, whole or as peanut butter. Supplements of tryptophan have been taken off the shelves in the past due to product contamination. This was due to a manufacturing error by a Japanese corporation.

VALINE
Needed to regulate the metabolism. It is used to treat depression as it acts as a mild stimulant. Helps prevent neurological disorders and may play a role in managing multiple sclerosis, as it protects the myelin sheath surrounding nerve fibres in the brain and spinal cord.

——7——
The Essential Fatty Acids

The amount of essential fatty acids (EFAs) in the body directly depends on how many fats and oils we eat in our diet. Fatty acids are the major building blocks of the fats in human beings and of the fats and oils in foods. They are an important source of energy for the body. Essential fatty acids also make up the majority of the protective envelope or membrane that surrounds every one of our cells. Although essential fatty acids are found in many foods, the most common sources are vegetable oils and fish oils.

Scientifically speaking, a fatty acid molecule is composed of two parts, one fatty and the other acid. Linked together, they become one fatty acid. Fatty acids consist of a chain of carbon and hydrogen atoms. The length of the chain determines the fatty acids' properties and use in the body. There are both long chain and short chain fatty acids. The shortest chains are around four carbons long, such as butyric acid, found in butter. The longest chains are around twenty-four carbons long, such as those found in fish oils and brain tissue.

Fatty acids have many different functions. They are used as part of our body fat, cushioning and protecting our internal organs. They are useful for shock absorption and also for producing energy. The shorter the chain of the fatty acids, the more easily it is digested in the body. This is important for those with a weak liver or gallbladder, who may find that they can eat butter but not smoked mackerel. The most important essential fatty acids are divided into two main families. The omega 3 family of alpha-linolenic acid and the omega 6 family of linoleic acid. Both these essential fatty acids are the 'parent' substances which are converted by the body into several other important fatty acids.

OMEGA 3 FATTY ACIDS

Alpha-linolenic acid, commonly called linolenic acid, is found in linseed oil, pumpkin seeds, soya beans, walnuts and dark green leaves.

Eicosapentaeonic acid (EHA) and docosahexaenoic acid (DHA) can also be made to a limited extent in the body from alpha-linolenic acid. Although EPA and DHA are mainly found in fish, certain parts of animals are also high in these specific fatty acids, including eyeballs, brain, testes and adrenal glands (perhaps why primitive cultures consider these parts to be such great delicacies). Although they are not strictly essential fatty acids, low levels of EPA and DHA in the diet can cause serious health problems. They are needed for many functions within the body, including the development and health of the eyes and brain. These oils can also help with inflammatory disorders, such as arthritis, and help to reduce a form of blood fats called triglycerides, which are linked to heart disease and strokes. This is why cod liver oil is taken to bring relief from arthritis and also why fish oils are available on prescription for the treatment and prevention of heart disease.

The symptoms of alpha-linolenic acid deficiency include eye disorders, stunted growth, muscle weakness, tingling in the arms and legs and behavioural changes. Those on very low-fat diets, or who do not eat any of the foods rich in alpha-linolenic acid (including fish or fish oils such as cod liver oil) may risk a deficiency which could led to health problems.

The richest source of fish oils are found in darkly coloured, oily fish. White-fleshed fish and shellfish have the lowest levels of beneficial fish oils.

Fish rich in omega-3 EFAs (in order):
Mackerel
Herrings
Sardines
*Bluefin tuna **
Lake trout
Salmon
Anchovies
Sprats
Mullet
Halibut
Bass
Rainbow trout
Carp
Squid

* Tuna should be bought fresh and not tinned as the natural fish oil is drained off and replaced with refined vegetable oil or brine.

OMEGA 6 FATTY ACIDS

The parent essential fatty acid of this group is linolenic acid, which is found in vegetable oils, including safflower, soybean, walnut, pumpkin seed, sesame seed and flax. Safflower oil is the richest source of linolenic acid, although some highly bred commercial varieties contain only small quantities of linolenic acid. Linolenic acid can be converted by the body into gamma-linolenic acid (GLA) which is also naturally found in a few sources, including breast milk, evening primrose oil, borage or starflower oil and blackcurrant-seed oil. Gamma-linolenic acid is widely documented to help those with atopic eczema and symptoms of PMS, including severe breast pain. A supplement containing a standardized form of the essential fatty acid GLA is available on prescription from GPs to treat these conditions.

Supplements of evening primrose oil and other GLA-rich oils are also taken to relieve dry skin conditions and preserve the fatty membranes that surround skin cells.

Symptoms of linolenic acid deficiency include eczema-like skin disorders, hair loss, liver problems, behavioural disturbances, dry body fluids, sterility, heart disorders and growth retardation. A diet very low in fat or without any source of linolenic acid can cause serious health problems.

SATURATED FATS
Some fatty acids are 'saturated', meaning that they are fully saturated with as many hydrogen atoms as they can possibly contain. Saturated fats are high in stearic acid, found in large amounts in beef, lamb and pork. Palmitic acid is also a saturated fatty acid and is found in tropical oils, including coconut and palm oils. Although these tropical oils are of vegetable origin they are high in unhealthy saturated fatty acids. All saturated fats should be reduced in our diet. They are responsible for clogging our arteries and disrupting healthy hormone activity. Most foods now carry labelling which states their saturated fat content. However, beware of 'hidden' fats, such as animal fats and tropical oils commonly added to cakes, biscuits and cereals. It is worth getting into the habit of reading the label before you buy to check first the product's fat content, and secondly the type of fat that it contains.

POLYUNSATURATED FATS
Chemically speaking, polyunsaturated fats have the fewest hydrogen atoms linked to their chains of carbon molecules. Polyunsaturated fats, such as safflower or sunflower oil, reduce the levels of harmful LDL (low density lipoproteins) in the bloodstream. These blood fats are responsible for depositing cholesterol in the arteries. However, more recent research has shown that polyunsaturated fats may have the unwanted side-

effect of reducing levels of the beneficial blood fats called HDL (high density lipoproteins). The normal ratio of HDL to LDL is thought to be 1:5, which means that the HDL has to work hard to carry the cholesterol away from our cells. Too many polyunsaturated fats may upset this delicate balance. We should also be aware that the more polyunsaturated fats we eat, the more vitamin E we need in our diet. This is because the vitamin E acts as an antioxidant within the fats in our cells and prevents these fats from oxidizing, or turning rancid.

MONOUNSATURATED FATS

The monounsaturated fats are unsaturated fatty acids with one double bond (hence 'mono', meaning single). The most important monounsaturated fatty acid in nutrition is called oleic acid. In technical terms, it has an eighteen-carbon chain with one double bond always between carbons nine and ten. Oleic acid is found in olive oil, almond oil and other seed oils. It is also found in the membranes of plant and animal cells and helps to keep the arteries and skin supple. Monounsaturates are stable at high temperatures (so olive oil is good for cooking) and are not believed to disrupt the balance of HDL:LDL in the same way that polyunsaturated fats can. In Mediterranean countries, where plenty of olive oil, olives, avocados and nuts are eaten, there are much lower rates of coronary heart disease and cancer. These are widely attributed to the monounsaturated fats found in all these foods.

——— 8 ———
The Antioxidant ACE Vitamins

The most exciting discovery in recent years has been that one of the most important combinations of vitamins is the A, C and E or 'ACE' vitamins (vitamin A in the form of beta-carotene, found in colourful fruit and vegetables) combination. All three nutrients act as powerful antioxidants. This means that they are capable of protecting the body from the damage caused by an excess of free radicals. The free radicals are super-charged, highly aggressive particles of oxygen which are constantly being created inside the body. As you read this sentence thousands more free radicals are being released. The ACE vitamins are able to neutralize these particles before they can damage our cells.

Large amounts of free radicals are highly damaging within the body, although a small number are usefully employed in fighting bacteria and viruses. Problems occur when the amounts of free radicals generated get out of control and they start attacking the body. Free radicals are essentially molecular fragments with an unpaired electron. This makes them highly unstable. Because electrons prefer to go around in pairs, they try and 'grab' another electron from a passing molecule to pair up. A free radical is a loose-living electron playing the field for a mate to settle down with. Unfortunately, it breaks up other pairs to find a partner and creates many more unstable molecules in the process. In short, a chain reaction occurs within the body which damages our cells.

In addition to the ACE vitamins there is a group of minerals that helps in the fight against free radicals. In fact, the body's first line of defence in fighting the damage caused by free radicals comes from a group of enzymes that contains the minerals manganese, copper, zinc and selenium. One of these, SOD (superoxide dismutase) is at the forefront of both heart disease and cancer research. Another close relative antioxidant enzyme, GP (glutathione peroxidase) also shows promise as a potential cancer preventer. Enzymes control all the chemical changes that take place in our cells, including the creation and release of energy that keeps the body ticking. Enzymes are catalysts, so they work by speeding up chemical changes that take place in our cells. But they need to be triggered to work. Part of the work done by these minerals inside the body is to boost the action of various enzymes.

There is no doubt that we all need to protect ourselves from free-radical damage by eating more antioxidants. Free-radical damage is widespread through the body and is now believed to play a major part in heart disease. It is also linked to diabetes, cataracts, arthritis, skin wrinkling and even the very ageing process itself. The antioxidants are the ideal weapons for our body to fight the damage done by too many free radicals. Eating large amounts of foods rich in beta-carotene, vitamin C and vitamin E is essential for good health – although some of the quantities are simply staggering. For example, you need to munch your way through almost a kilo of apricots to provide 15mg of beta-carotene, over a kilo of potatoes to give 100mg of vitamin C and almost four kilos of butter to provide 75mg of vitamin E! The more sensible way to boost antioxidant supplies is with a daily supplement. This is especially important if you are exposed to factors that encourage an excess of free radicals. These include ultra-violet sunshine, smoking, pollution from car exhaust fumes and solvents.

—— 9 ——
Special Needs for Vitamins and Minerals

Babies

New mothers are bombarded with advice about healthy feeding, but one thing is clear – children are never too young to start receiving vitamins and minerals in their diet. All formula baby milks are fortified with a complex blend of synthetic vitamins and minerals to help promote growth and good health. Breast milk often contains more natural vitamins and minerals, depending on the mother's diet. If the mother takes sensible levels of supplements or eats more wholesome foods, her milk will be more nutritious. Breast milk also contains many other factors not found in formula milks, including the essential fatty acids EPA, DHA and GLA, as well as natural growth factors and protective antibodies. This is why the *Breast is Best* slogan is still true for infant feeding and there is a long way to go before powdered formula milks become as good as breast milk.

The Health Education Authority recommends giving a child supplementary vitamin drops as soon as it is weaned from breast or formula milk on to cows' milk. This is because cows' milk does not contain as many nutrients as breast or formula milks. These vitamin drops should be given until the age of two, and preferably until the child is five years old. Vitamin drops for babies and small children are widely available from chemists and at reduced cost from local authority child-care clinics. Vitamin drops are also available free of charge for all those on income support. The drops are not a substitute for eating well as they contain only the vitamins A, C and D. These are the vitamins that are also found in cod liver oil, another popular children's supplement. However, it is important not to give the vitamin drops in addition to large amounts of cod liver oil, as you will be doubling the dose of vitamin D which is not desirable. For my own children, I prefer to give them flavoured cod liver oil instead of vitamin drops. This is because it contains the essential fatty acids EPA and DHA as well as the vitamins, but this is a personal choice.

The other main nutrient likely to be lacking in a baby's diet is iron. All babies are born with a good supply of iron and when this is added to the iron they automatically receive from breast or formula milk, their supplies will last until they are five or six months old. After this time, babies will need to be given foods containing iron. These include sieved green vegetables such as spinach or well-cooked egg yolks. Do not give iron supplements to babies or small children as it is easy to give too much and an overdose can cause permanent damage.

Some other supplements may be useful as children get bigger. For example, chewable vitamin C tablets are useful for those children who don't eat oranges or drink fresh fruit juices. Liquid calcium supplements are useful for babies and small children who are on a dairy-free diet. Calcium is vitally important in the first few years of life to build strong bones and if your child does not eat dairy products due to an allergy, he or she must be given extra calcium supplies. Try to include as many fresh fruits, vegetables and whole grains in a child's daily diet. Dried fruit is also a useful substitute for sugary snacks, and diluted fruit juices such as apple or orange are good alternatives to synthetic squashes or fizzy drinks. Children who go through a phase of not eating vegetables can be given carrot juice to drink (or mix it in with other foods) as this is a very rich source of beta-carotene, an important antioxidant nutrient.

Children

The jury is still out on whether extra vitamin supplies can improve a child's intelligence or not. Some clinical trials suggest that they do, a few have found that they do not. However, studies have shown that children who were given vitamin supplements out-performed those who were given placebo (dummy) pills. Those taking the vitamins showed an improvement equivalent to more than four IQ points, regardless of age, sex or original IQ of the child. Unfortunately, these results have not been repeated, although trials are currently underway to try and determine the exact effect of vitamins on childhood intelligence. Meanwhile, more recent research at the Dunn Nutrition Centre in Cambridge has shown that babies who were breastfed have a higher IQ level by the time they are eight years old. The average increase is around 6 IQ points. This is possibly due to the increased vitamins, minerals and essential fatty acids responsible for brain development that the child received in the first few months of life.

All children require good levels of vitamins and minerals to build strong, healthy bodies. It is a parent's duty to make sure his/her children receive the basic building-blocks for good health. Breakfast is an important meal for children as it keeps their energy levels high and helps them concentrate during the morning hours at school. Most breakfast cereals are fortified with additional vitamins and minerals. However, these are only fortified with a few nutrients, and even then only at a small percentage of the already low RDAs (the minimum amounts to prevent illness from deficiency). One bowl of low-sugar breakfast cereal is a good start to the day, but it will not give children all they need to see them through the day. Breakfast cereals can be supplemented with chopped fruit, such as apple or banana, and served with fruit juice as a way of giving extra vitamin supplies. If your child eats junk food for lunch or tea it is worth trying to sneak in healthier alternatives, such as dried fruit, carrot sticks with dips, peanut-butter sandwiches on wholemeal bread, low-fat yoghurts and fresh fruit salad. Constant 'grazing' on high-fat, sugary or salty snacks throughout the day can take away a child's appetite for more nutritious main meals. If you suspect that your child may not be getting its fair share of nutrients, a children's vitamin and mineral supplement is a good option.

Teenagers

The body places tremendous demands on teenagers. Not only are they under a great deal of stress from exams and first love, but this is also a time when they are physically changing due to puberty. It is not unusual for a teenager to grow 10cms in height or add more than five kilos in body weight in a year. These dramatic changes need to be fuelled by the best form of nutrition. Active adolescent boys may need up to 4,000 calories a day (twice the normal adult man's recommended intake). Less active boys who spend more time playing computer games than sport will obviously need less than this, as do teenage girls. But good levels of vitamins and minerals are essential at this important stage in human growth and development.

Teenage bodies need high intakes of good-quality protein, such as fish, eggs, meat and nuts to ensure healthy muscle growth. Both boys and girls require good supplies of iron for the increased muscle development and blood supply. Foods rich in iron include dark green leafy vegetables, red meat, eggs, beans and lentils. Teenage girls may need extra iron supplements if they have heavy periods as a lot of iron is lost in the blood. Supplements can also be a useful nutritional insurance policy for teenagers. This can be especially important if a teenager is on a slimming diet, any kind of food fad or is a fussy eater.

Vegetarians will also benefit from supplements as often a teenager who becomes a vegetarian will simply cut out all animal produce without replacing it with nutritionally sound alternatives.

Vegetarians

Anyone following a restricted diet needs to be aware of their daily nutrient intake. Vegetarians and even stricter vegans can risk deficiencies of protein, iron, zinc and vitamin B12. Vegetarians should also vary their foods to obtain the maximum amount of protein. This should come from pulses such as beans and lentils, nuts, seeds and wholegrain cereals. The most useful form of iron (haem iron) is found in red meat. Vegetarians who rely on plant sources of iron (non-haem iron), such as green leafy vegetables, should also eat plenty of vitamin C to increase its absorption. Red meat is also one of the most common sources of vitamin B12 so vegetarians should include fortified breakfast cereals, Marmite and other yeast extract products which are rich in vitamin B12 in their diet. In addition, the best sources of zinc also come from animal produce. Vegetarians often have low intakes of zinc and should consider a daily supplement. As vitamin D is only available in food from animal produce (such as cod liver oil) it is important to eat fortified foods, such as breakfast cereals and margarine. Another way to receive vitamin D is through the action of sunlight on the skin, so those who spend some time outdoors everyday will not be deficient.

Dairy produce is also a useful source of calcium and vitamin D, so vegans or other people who restrict their intake of milk, butter and cheese should consider taking a calcium supplement. Soya products, such as soya milk, yoghurt and cheese, are a good option, provided that they have been specifically enriched with calcium (check the label before buying). Other excellent vegetarian sources of calcium are green leafy vegetables, nuts and seeds (especially sesame seeds if you eat enough of them). Although vegetables and whole grains are very nutritious and an excellent part of the vegetarian diet, be aware that high fibre foods tend to bind with minerals in the intestines, making them less available to the body. The main culprits are wheat bran and wheat fibre, which is why adding spoonfuls of plain bran to the diet is not such a good idea. Those on a high-fibre diet may find a calcium and zinc supplement useful.

Adults

By the time we have grown up, our eating patterns have been firmly established and it is hard to break unhealthy habits. Despite the vast amount of information about healthy eating that is available to us, the majority continue to eat a diet low in essential vitamins and minerals. Eating more fruits and vegetables is an easy, cheap and convenient way to boost our daily nutrition. Unfortunately, studies show that many of us spend more on alcohol and cigarettes than we do on fruit and vegetables. For example, in Scotland, a third of all adults do not eat enough fresh produce to supply their daily vitamin and mineral needs. This lack of a well-balanced diet could be one reason why Scotland tops the European table for deaths due to heart disease.

Eating well takes on more significance as we grow older and the main life-threatening diseases loom on the horizon. Fortunately, many studies are now showing that those with a diet high in antioxidant nutrients (such as vitamins C, E and beta-carotene) are better protected against some cancers and heart disease. Not only should we eat more of these nutrients in our food, but we should also watch out for other lifestyle factors that can use up our supplies within the body. Factors that can interfere with the absorption of vital vitamins include drinking too much tea and coffee (and other drinks containing caffeine), taking drugs (including prescription medicines) and stress at all levels. Smoking and drinking alcohol both use up precious vitamins and minerals. If you smoke or drink, it is well worth considering taking supplements to put nutrients back into the system. The antioxidant nutrients are especially valuable for those who do not eat much fresh fruit or vegetables, or who live or work in a polluted environment.

Vitamins Against the Effects of Smoking

Much research has been carried out to see if vitamins can protect smokers. The damaging effects of smoking are well known and smoking causes one-third of all deaths in middle age, killing one person every five minutes. The metal ions in cigarette smoke destroy our levels of vitamin C. Each cigarette wipes out around 2.5mg of vitamin C, roughly equivalent to the amount found in a small orange. For this reason, smokers risk not having enough vitamin C to remain healthy. Very low levels of vitamin C have been found in the bloodstream of smokers, which may be one reason why they are more likely to develop infections, including coughs, colds and 'flu. Those who smoke also have less beta-carotene and vitamin E in their bloodstream. These are also antioxidant nutrients, so those who do smoke (or who live or work with a smoker) should consider increasing the levels of vitamin C, beta-carotene and vitamin E in their diet.

Vitamins for Beauty

Vitamins not only help keep us healthy, they go a long way to build the body beautiful too. A diet rich in vital vitamins and minerals is one of the best ways to ward off wrinkles and encourage stronger hair and skin. The antioxidants are also an essential part of anti-ageing as they help prevent the damage caused by free radicals that leads to skin wrinkling and sagging. The antioxidant vitamins C and E are especially useful for protecting the skin from free-radical attack. Look closely at any jar of skin cream and you will see that they are now added to help fight the effects of ageing from the outside as well as from within.

SKIN

Vitamin C is needed to create healthy collagen, the protein that keeps our complexion supple and smooth. The formation of collagen is entirely dependent on vitamin C because a substance called hydroxyproline (made by vitamin C and the amino acid proline) is the major constituent of collagen. Vitamin C and bioflavonoids are also needed to strengthen capillary walls and keep blood vessels in the skin healthy. Beta-carotene and vitamin E are also important anti-ageing antioxidants for the skin. This means that they can help prevent the free-radical damage that interferes with healthy skin cell turnover and leads to premature lines, wrinkles, skin slackening and sagging. Other nutrients that are especially useful for building and maintaining strong, supple skin are vitamin A, biotin, pantothenic acid, silicon and zinc.

NAILS

Beta-carotene helps to fortify nails and can help prevent flaking and splitting. Nail ridges can be caused by low levels of the B complex vitamins, while white spots on the surface of the nail can be due to insufficient zinc in the diet. Strong, flexible nails can also be encouraged by increasing the amount of essential fatty acids in the diet. This means using vegetable oils, such as sunflower or olive oil when cooking, or taking capsules of evening primrose oil or cod liver oil.

Hair

We need a steady supply of protein and minerals to keep our hair shiny and strong. The B complex vitamins, notably pantothenic acid and vitamin B12, together with zinc and selenium are particularly important for healthy hair growth and for helping to prevent hair loss. Pantothenic acid in the form of panthenol is often added to shampoos and hair conditioners to encourage shiny, more manageable hair. Top dog breeders give their show dogs cod liver oil to maintain a glossy coat – and this can also have a similar effect for humans! Increasing the levels of essential fatty acids in the diet, with either supplements or vegetable oils in cooking, helps promote healthier hair.

Pregnancy

The nine months of pregnancy make unique demands on the body. Not only does the pregnant women have to feed herself, she is also providing the nourishment for another rapidly growing person. Not surprisingly, this is an important time to keep nutrient levels high. It is during the first three months of pregnancy that all the baby's organs are formed, making optimum nutrition essential. Even during the first few days of pregnancy the foetus is undergoing rapid change and development. This is at a time when most women do not even know they are pregnant. For this reason it is well worth following a healthy diet and lifestyle when planning for pregnancy and before conception. Avoid drinking alcohol, smoking and consider taking additional vitamin and mineral supplements – especially folic acid. This nutrient has been shown to reduce the risk of spina bifida in babies. However, it should literally be taken from day one of conception. By about the twelfth week of pregnancy the baby's neural tubes are fully closed and so the nutrient cannot offer any protection after this time. If there is a chance that you might become pregnant it is important to take folic acid supplements (see page 24).

Unfortunately, although the best nutrition is needed during the first few months of pregnancy this is also a time when morning sickness strikes. Even though you may feel too sick or tired to eat properly it is well worth stocking the fridge with nutritious foods. Eating little and often is often helpful and can keep nausea at bay. A well-balanced vitamin and mineral supplement is also a good idea – although all pregnant women should limit their intake of vitamin A (retinol) and avoid eating liver or liver products such as pâté (see Vitamin A on page 18). Many pregnant women are also advised by their doctors to take iron supplements. These help to prevent anaemia, which in a mild form may be present in a third of all pregnant women, both during and after pregnancy. Most pregnant women feel tired, especially during the last few months, which is another reason why it is important to avoid running short of iron.

Good nutrition for the mum-to-be and her baby does not stop at childbirth! Every woman needs an especially healthy post-baby diet. This is because many of her vital vitamin and mineral reserves will have been used up during the last few months of pregnancy. A well-balanced diet will also supply the new mother with essential nutrients needed to help cope with the new demands of the body. The B complex vitamins and zinc have been shown to be helpful in combating post-natal depression or common baby blues. Extra supplies of vitamins and minerals are also needed for those wonderful women who choose to breastfeed. Bear in mind when breast feeding that the content of your milk reflects your diet. Those who don't eat well produce thin milk which is less nutritious than those who eat plenty of nutritious foods and take additional supplements. Breast milk is also uniquely rich in the essential fatty acid GLA, which is important for the baby's healthy development. By eating plenty of fish and seafood you will also pass on the essential fatty acids EPA and DHA, which are especially important for developing healthy brain tissue.

Menopause

A woman's needs change during the menopause as the body releases more calcium from the bones. This is due to the change in oestrogen supply just before and after the menopause. A diet rich in calcium is believed to help compensate for this loss, and may also help prevent osteoporosis. This disease is also called brittle bone disorder, as it weakens the skeleton and leads to bones which fracture and break much more easily. Osteoporosis can also lead to shortening of the spine, which results in the unattractive 'dowager's hump' or curvature of the spine common in older women. When increasing the amount of calcium in the diet (either through foods or supplements) it is important also to increase the levels of vitamin D. This is because vitamin D is needed to properly absorb and utilize calcium in the bones. The best sources of vitamin D are oily fish (such as mackerel) and margarine, which is artificially fortified. Cod liver oil is also a useful supplement as it contains high levels of vitamin D as well as other useful essential fatty acids. Women seeking to minimize the risk of osteoporosis could consider a daily supplement programme that includes a multi-vitamin and mineral tablet, with additional vitamin C with bioflavonoids, calcium, boron and zinc.

The Elderly

Those in their later years of life are more likely to suffer from poorer nutrition than the rest of the population. This may be due to low income, illness, loss of appetite, or mental or physical lethargy in meal preparation. Many old people living on their own simply don't bother to cook meals for one and live on an assortment of processed foods. They are also more likely to indulge a sweet tooth by eating large amounts of sweet pastries, cakes and biscuits. While these are fine for an occasional treat, it is important not to fill up on high-sugar, high-fat foods that leave little room for anything more nutritious.

As the appetite decreases with age we need to make sure that the elderly receive their fair share of nutrients. This is especially important as some of the body's needs for vitamins and minerals increase during old age. In addition, many of the antioxidant nutrients such as beta-carotene and vitamins C and E have been shown to help prevent many of the diseases associated with old age. These include not only some forms of cancer and heart disease, but also arthritis, cataracts and strokes. Supplementing the diet with additional antioxidants is a sensible precaution, especially as many of the elderly are unwilling or simply unable to chew their way through large quantities of fresh fruits and vegetables. As the elderly are also more likely to be housebound or simply spend more time indoors they may not receive enough vitamin D through the action of sunlight on the skin. In this case, a daily vitamin D supplement or cod liver oil capsules can be useful.

Supplement Safety

When choosing a vitamin and mineral supplement follow these commonsense guidelines:

* Look for well-known brand names as these are manufactured to strict pharmaceutical standards.
* Take only the amount recommended on the pack.
* Only give children supplements that have been specifically formulated for them as the adult dosage may be too high.
* Pregnant women should limit their intake of vitamin A as mega-doses have been linked with birth defects.
* Choose natural source vitamins where possible as these are better absorbed and utilized by the body. These contain nutrients entirely extracted from natural foods, such as fruits, vegetables, seaweed, herbs, olive oil, soya bean and fish oils.
* Before conception and for twelve weeks afterwards, follow Government guidelines and take a daily folic acid supplement.
* Store supplements out of the reach of children.
* Take supplements with food when possible to increase their absorption.
* Always seek professional guidance when looking to treat medical disorders with a higher than usual therapeutic dose.

Vitamin and Mineral Food Tables

All foods are cooked unless otherwise stated; all fruits are raw.

Where to find vitamin A

FOOD	[MCG PER 100G (4OZ)]
Calves' liver	39,780mcg
Lamb's liver	22,680mcg
Cod liver oil	18,000mcg
Butter	815mcg
Margarine	780mcg
Cheese (eg Cheddar)	325mcg
Eggs	190mcg

Where to find beta-carotene

FOOD	[MCG PER 100G (4OZ)]
Carrots	4,425mcg
Parsley (raw)	4,040mcg
Sweet potatoes	3,960mcg
Spinach	3,840mcg
Watercress (raw)	2,520mcg
Spring greens	2,270mcg
Cantaloupe melon	1,000mcg
Tomatoes	640mcg
Asparagus	530mcg
Broccoli	475mcg
Apricots	405mcg
Peaches	58mcg

Where to find vitamin B1 (thiamine)

FOOD	[MG PER 100G (4OZ)]
Dried brewer's yeast	15.6mg
Wheatgerm	2.0mg
Oats	0.9mg
Pork	0.8mg
Nuts (eg hazelnuts)	0.4mg
Wholemeal bread	0.3mg

Where to find vitamin B2 (riboflavin)

FOOD	[MG PER 100G (4OZ)]
Yeast extract	11mg
Lamb's liver	4.4mg
Calves' liver	4.2mg
Baker's yeast	4mg
Wheatgerm	0.72mg
Cheese (eg Cheddar)	0.4mg
Wheat bran	0.36mg
Eggs	0.35mg
Soya beans	0.27mg
Yoghurt, plain	0.27mg
Broccoli	0.05mg

Where to find vitamin B3 (niacin)

FOOD	[MG PER 100G (4OZ)]
Yeast extract	58mg
Wheat bran	30mg
Pig's liver	11mg
Mackerel	10mg
Chicken	8mg
Beef steak	6mg
Wholemeal bread	4mg
Soya beans	2mg
Raisins	0.6mg

Where to find vitamin B5 (pantothenic acid)

FOOD	[MG PER 100G (4OZ)]
Baker's yeast	11mg
Pig's liver	5mg
Wheatgerm	2mg
Nuts (eg walnuts)	2mg
Chicken	1.2mg
Oats	1.2mg
Eggs	1.3mg
Beef steak	1.0mg
Soya beans	0.8mg

Where to find vitamin B6 (pyridoxine)

FOOD	[MG PER 100G (4OZ)]
Wheatgerm	3.3mg
Oats	3.3mg
Baker's yeast	2.0mg
Yeast extract	1.3mg
Mackerel	1.03mg
Pig's liver	0.64mg
Nuts (eg hazelnuts)	0.59mg
Lamb's liver	0.49mg
Soya beans	0.38mg
Potatoes	0.33mg
Bananas	0.29mg
Eggs	0.12mg

Where to find vitamin B9 (folic acid)

FOOD	[MCG PER 100G (4OZ)]
Baker's yeast	400mcg
Soya beans	370mcg
Wheatgerm	331mcg
Chick peas	180mcg
Green leafy vegetables (eg spinach)	150mcg
Lentils	110mcg
Pig's liver	110mcg
Oats	60mcg
Nuts (eg almonds)	48mcg
Wholemeal bread	39mcg
Cheese (eg Cheddar)	33mcg
Bananas	33mcg
Oranges	31mcg

Where to find vitamin B12 (cobalamin)

FOODS	[MCG PER 100G (4OZ)]
Pig's liver	26mcg
Pig's kidney	15mcg
Mackerel	6mcg
Lamb	2mcg
Pork	2mcg
Beef	2mcg
Fish	2mcg
Eggs	1.1mcg
Cheddar cheese	1.1mcg
Full-fat milk	0.4mcg

Where to find biotin

FOOD	[MCG PER 100G (4OZ)]
Baker's yeast	200mcg
Pig's kidney	53mcg
Pig's liver	34mcg
Wheatgerm	25mcg
Oats	21mcg
Eggs	16mcg
Wholemeal bread	6mcg
Mackerel	3mcg
Milk	2mcg

Where to find vitamin C

FOOD	[MG PER 100G (4OZ)]
Guavas	230mg
Blackcurrants	200mg
Parsley (raw)	190mg
Green peppers (raw)	120mg
Strawberries	77mg
Kale	71mg
Watercress (raw)	62mg
Brussels sprouts	60mg
Lemons	58mg
Oranges	54mg
Broccoli	44mg
Tomato purée	38mg
Grapefruit	36mg
Cauliflower	27mg
Red cabbage	20mg
Baked potatoes (with skin)	14mg
Bananas	11mg
Apples	6mg

Where to find vitamin D

FOOD	[MCG PER 100G (4OZ)]
Cod liver oil	210mcg
Kippers	25mcg
Tinned salmon	13mcg
Mackerel	8mcg
Margarine	8mcg
Tinned sardines	8mcg
Eggs	2mcg

Where to find vitamin E

FOOD	[MG PER 100G (4OZ)]
Wheatgerm oil *	136mg
Sunflower oil *	49mg
Safflower oil *	40mg
Sunflower seeds	38mg
Almonds	24mg
Wheatgerm	22mg
Cod liver oil	20mg
Peanut oil *	15mg
Tomato purée	5.3mg
Olive oil *	5.1mg
Peanut butter	5.0mg
Egg yolks	3.1mg
Potato crisps	3.1mg
Spinach	1.7mg
Soya beans	1.1mg
Roasted peanuts	1.1mg
Asparagus	1.1mg

* Unrefined vegetable oils contain higher levels of vitamin E. The vitamin E content of oils declines during cooking.

Where to find calcium

FOOD	[MG PER 100G (4OZ)]
Cheddar cheese	720mg
Sesame seeds	670mg
Tinned sardines	550mg
Yoghurt	200mg
Spinach	160mg
Skimmed milk	120mg
Full-fat milk	115mg
Sunflower seeds	110mg
Cream cheese	98mg
Nuts	78mg
Chick peas	46mg
Broccoli	40mg

Where to find magnesium

FOOD	[MG PER 100G (4OZ)]
Brazil nuts	410mg
Almonds	270mg
Cashew nuts	250mg
Baker's yeast	230mg
Peanuts	180mg
Wholemeal bread	76mg
Soya beans	63mg
Shrimps	49mg
Brown rice	43mg
Raisins	35mg
Bananas	34mg
Peas	21mg